ABLED

BY SAHARA-DUNE MUNUO JOHN

"INSPIRING CELEBRITIES WITH DISABILITIES ...
ANYTHING'S POSSIBLE!"

SunCyclebooks.com

"INSPIRING CELEBRITIES WITH DISABILITIES ...
ANYTHING'S POSSIBLE!"

ABLED: Inspiring Celebrities With Disabilities
by Sahara-Dune Munuo John

First publication December 2017
With the services of: Sun Cycle Publishers

e: SunCycleBooks@mail.com
w: SunCycleBooks.com

This Publication employs archival-quality paper
and meets all ANSI standards for archival quality paper.

Reproduction only with written email permission from the Author.
Parts of this book may however be used only in reference
to support related documents or subjects.

INTRODUCTION

Hi, my name is Sahara Dune. I live in London.

I am 13 years old and I have a disability, which basically means that some of my muscles don't work fully. I decided to write this book to let people know that even though people are disabled, it doesn't stop us doing great things!.

I want to help people have a better life even though they are disabled. This book is about inspirational celebrities who all have some kind of disability, and this has not stopped them from doing great and amazing things - because anything's possible!.

Love. Sahara Dune :)

Kanya Sasser

Kanya Sasser hyperloop was born in Thailand. She was born with no legs, which hasn't stopped her from doing great things. She was left at a Buddhist temple as a baby and American family adopted her. She now lives in California.

She is very pretty and at the age of 15 started modelling sportswear. Kanya is a very sporty girl, she likes doing different exciting sports such as break dancing, skateboarding, surfing, mono-skiing, swimming, hiking, wheelchair racing, tennis, rugby and basketball.

Kanya is training to compete in the Winter Paralympic Games in mono-skiing.

Kanya Says:

"I've always had body confidence throughout my whole life. I just see i'm like everybody else. People are different, yes, and they do different things. I do life differently, I adapt in my own way and how I can."

- Kanya training for the Mono-ski Winter Paralympics.
- She loves skateboarding, and uses it instead of a wheelchair to get around.

She's extremely popular and has over 10,000 Instagram followers, and I am one of them!. Kanya chooses not to use a wheelchair, instead travels around California on her skateboard.

Kanya's inspiring because she is different and unique from everyone else, and has achieved amazing things her motto is "No legs, No limits!".

IDRIS ELBA

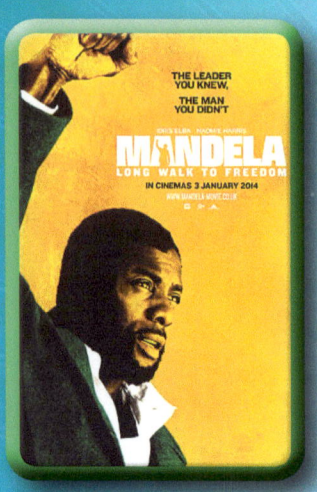

● (Above) Idris Elba acting as Nelson Mandela in the film: A Long Walk to Freedom.

● Idris speaking in the British Houses of Parliament about diversity and inclusion for people with disabilities.

Idris Elba is a British actor who has starred in many movies. He played Nelson Mandela in the film ' A Long Walk to Freedom.'

Idris also wrote, directed and acted in a short film called 'King for a Term' It is also his true childhood story.

When he was a kid he lived in Hackney, East London with his mum and dad, who are from Sierra Leone and Ghana, in Africa. Idris had problems breathing when he was a child called Asthmatic Lungs.

When he was 10 years old his school couldn't manage his asthma. This is a disability because he couldn't breath normally and had Asthma attacks. So he had to be sent for a term to Stormont House, a School for children with special needs. Because Idris was disabled himself when he was a boy, now that he's famous he isn't afraid to speak up!.

Idris Elba spoke in The Westminster Houses of Parliament in London, about inclusion for people with disabilities.

Idris Elber's short film: King for a Term.

Idris Says: "For one term I was sent to this school for kids with disabilities – my disability was Asthma. I learned a lot there – how to deal with different people and develop different skills. It was there that my personality opened and grew."

● Idris acting as his father!, in a short film for Channel 4. He wrote, acted and directed it. Called 'King for a Term' about his childhood.

ANNE WAFULA-STRIKE

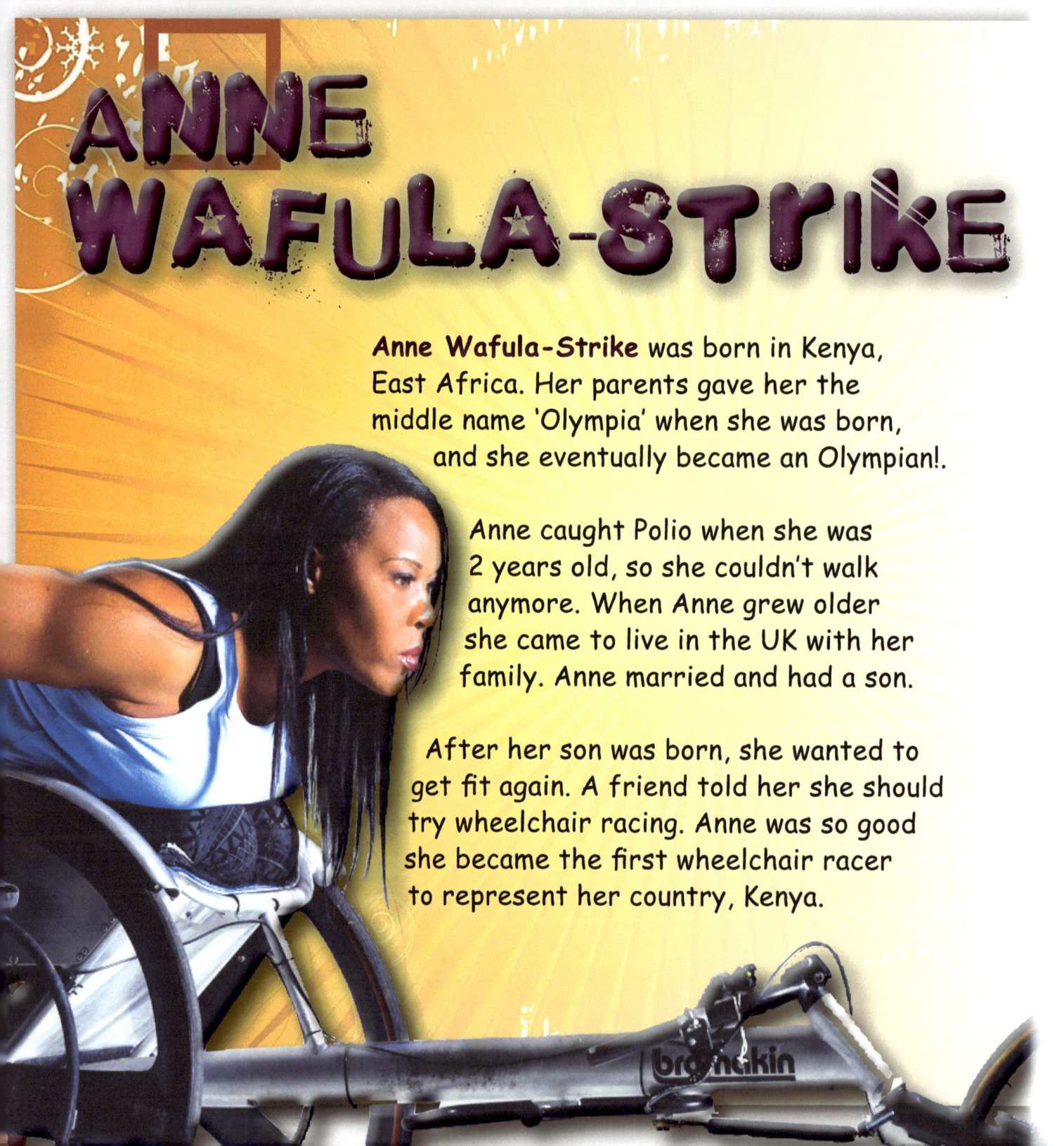

Anne Wafula-Strike was born in Kenya, East Africa. Her parents gave her the middle name 'Olympia' when she was born, and she eventually became an Olympian!.

Anne caught Polio when she was 2 years old, so she couldn't walk anymore. When Anne grew older she came to live in the UK with her family. Anne married and had a son.

After her son was born, she wanted to get fit again. A friend told her she should try wheelchair racing. Anne was so good she became the first wheelchair racer to represent her country, Kenya.

Then eventually for Great Britain. In 2012 she held the special Olympic torch in GB Olympic Games. Anne was also given a special award by the Queen of England for her achievements, called an MBE for special work for disability sport and charity.

Anne also wrote her very own book just like me! called **"In my Dreams I Dance."** The book is the story of her life. She now gives motivational talks and does charity work in Africa, and inspires people to do amazing things. I'm inspired by Anne because she's amazing!. She had a difficult life as a child, and that didn't stop her from achieving great things.

Anne Says: "I've tried so hard not to let my disability get in my way, I just get on with life. I try to lead a normal life, just like any other person, My life has been full and rich."

- Anne is the first person in Europe to do the "Tough Mudder" challenge in a wheelchair.
- Anne receiving an award, she competed for the GB Paralympics team.

ELLIE SIMMONDS

Ellie Simmonds is a Paralympic champion. She has won many gold medals for Great Britain. Ellie was born in the West Midlands, UK and became interested in swimming at the age of five.

Simmonds is a dwarf. A dwarf is someone who doesn't grow to full height. At 8 years old Ellie was sometimes even beating fully abled children in swimming competitions!.

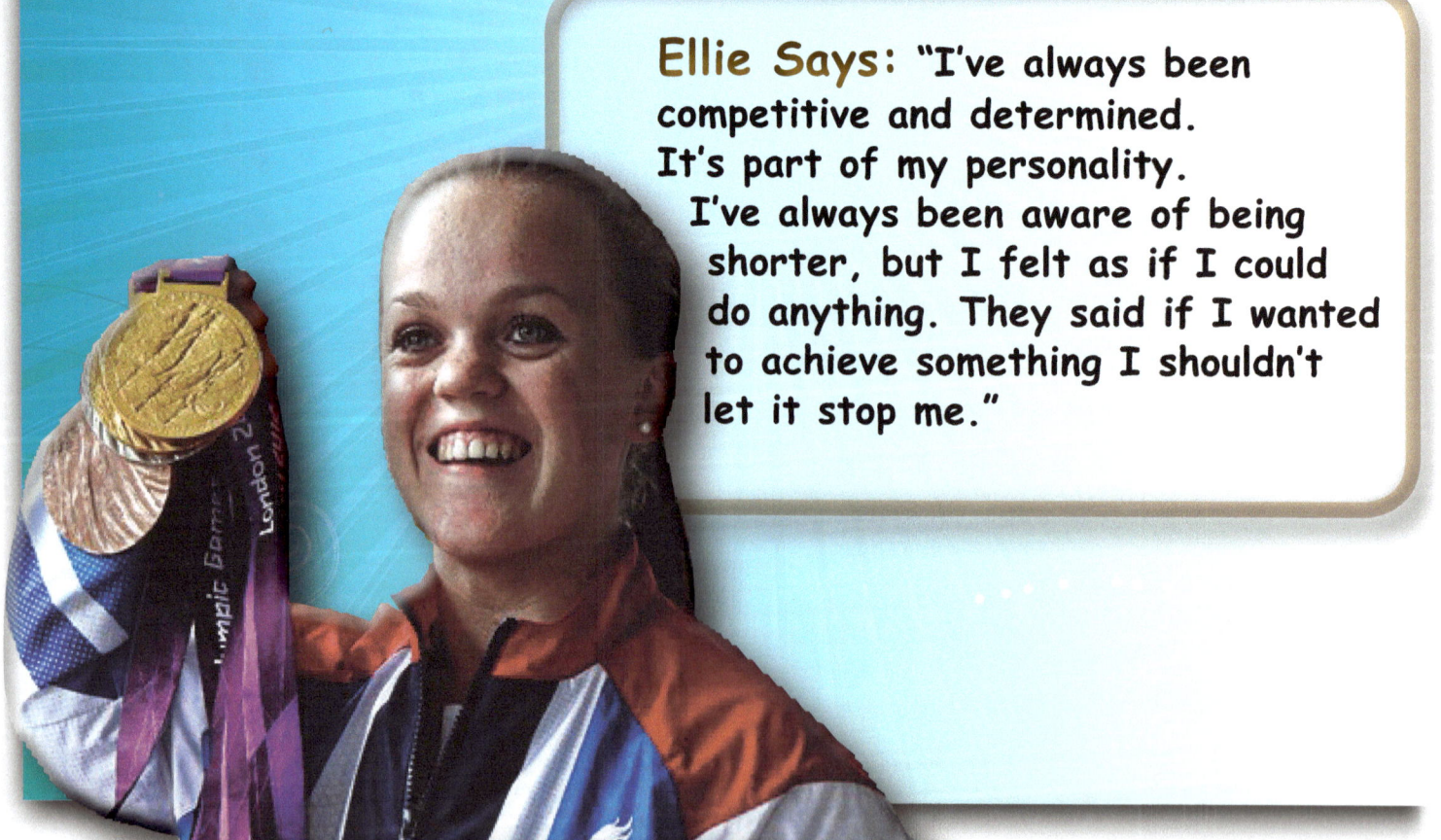

Ellie Says: "I've always been competitive and determined. It's part of my personality.
I've always been aware of being shorter, but I felt as if I could do anything. They said if I wanted to achieve something I shouldn't let it stop me."

She took part in the 2012 Summer Paralympic Games in London, and won 4 Olympic medals. Breaking her world record twice in the someday!

In 2009, The Queen also awarded Ellie an MBE for her achievements. At 14 she was the youngest ever to receive an MBE award.

Ellie is very determined and even though she's a disabled person she still did the things she wanted to achieve.

- Ellie swimming for team GB.
- Ellie receiving an award at Buckingham Palace.
- Young Ellie horse riding.

STEPHEN WILTSHIRE

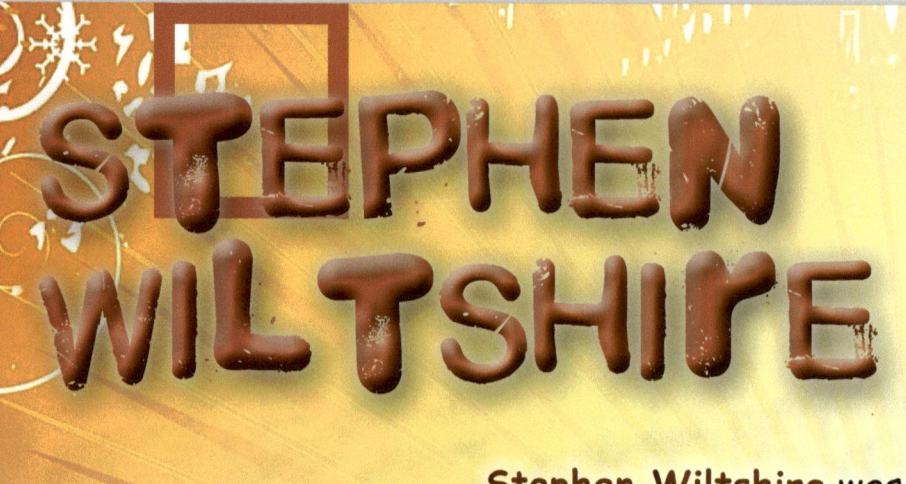

Stephen Wiltshire was born in London to Caribbean parents. His father is from Barbados and his mother from St. Lucia. Some of my family are from St Lucia too!. Stephen can't communicate very well, because he's Autistic. Autism is a condition that your born with, and it affects language skills and the way you behave.

Stephen Says: "I Have Never Seen Myself With a Disability, I Have Only Seen Myself As A POSSIBILITY. Being someone great and confident, spreading my love for drawing and only encouraging others to pursue your dreams regardless of whatever hurdles you may come across".

Stephen Wiltshire is sensational!, for the fact that his Autism hasn't stopped him from being very talented and creative.

Stephen really has an attention to detail, he uses his breathtaking photographic memory, to draw and create Architectural Art.

Stephen can just look at a landscape only once and can paint a picture from his memory of what he's seen. He draws entire cities, remembering every detail from short helicopter rides.

He has drawn many cities all over the world from memory on massive canvases. Stephen has drawn the cities of London, Tokyo, Rome, Hong Kong, Frankfurt, Madrid, Dubai, Jerusalem, Sydney, Shanghai, Brisbane, New York, Singapore and Istanbul. All from his memory!.

You can see his work permanently displayed at The Royal Opera Arcade in Central London, England.

- Stephen has a real life superpower!. He can draw from memory a landscape in detail after seeing it just

- In 2006, Wiltshire was given an MBE special award for services to art

CLAUDIA GORDON

Claudia Gordon was born in Jamaica, in the Caribbean, then moved to America as a child with her family. Claudia is the first deaf African-American female who graduated from university to become a lawyer. Even though Claudia couldn't hear, at 8 years old, she was determined to specialize in rights for people with disabilities. She's very inspirational to me because even though she is deaf, she still had the determination to achieve her goals. Claudia even had a job at President Obama's White House, as an adviser for the Disabled Community. Whether differently abled or not, you can still do great things. A disability can't stop you, anything's possible!

- Claudia working at President Obama's White House.
- Winner of Deaf Person of the year.

Claudia Says:

"I want to contribute to a better society where there is more understanding and acceptance of people with disabilities and where the same opportunities are provided for all. Also mentoring youth with disabilities keeps me motivated. I have an innate desire to give back. It is uplifting when you are able to empower another and help someone discover a sense of self-worth and confidence in their own abilities."

NICOLAS HAMILTON

● Nicolas with his big brother, Formula One champ Lewis Hamilton.

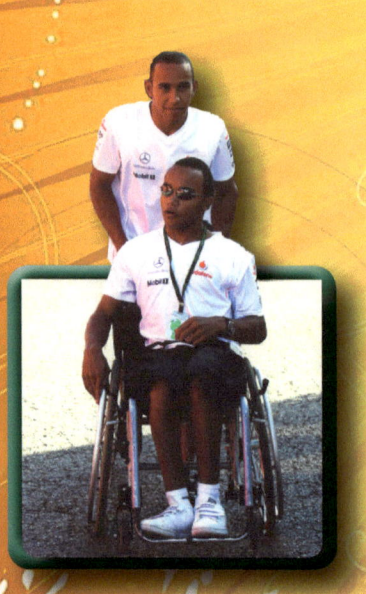

Nicholas Hamilton has Cerebral Palsy. I have Cerebral Palsy just like him. It's not stopped him from doing great things. It hasn't stopped him from training hard with The Disabled Motoring UK team.

He went on an epic and exciting challenge driving from the UK, through France and the Alps in Switzerland, on a mobility trike. He must have had a lot of fun!.

Nicholas Says:
"Your body is what it is, and it is your choice to use it to the best of your ability. If I am thinking I can't do it, then I push myself to give it a try, facing doubt with courage. It is what makes life exciting and enjoyable."

By the way Nicholas's brother is Lewis Hamilton, one of the greatest British Formula One drivers in the world, who dated the famous Nicole Scherzinger who was a judge on the X Factor, and belonged to the group called The Pussy Cat Dolls!.

Nicholas Hamilton is very brave and determined to make his dreams come true even though he isn't fully abled.

HELEN KELLER

Helen Keller grew up in Alabama, USA in the 1800's. She was deaf and blind.

She couldn't see, hear or talk. That didn't stop her from doing great things. She got a degree, became a global celebrity and taught in over 40 countries.

Ms. Sullivan was her dedicated teacher. She taught Helen many things. She helped Helen see her potential, teaching her how to spell, to speak and how to write, and read in 'Braille' (which is a way of reading for blind or visually impaired people), so she could communicate, read and write in a new way. She went on to write 12 books!. Helen is inspiring because she helped others like her who were also disabled.

She was also an activist. An activist is a person who protests for people to live better lives. Helen fought for the rights of people with disabilities, poor workers, women's rights and civil rights, supporting The NAACP (The National Association for the Advancement of Colored People) and The Suffragette's.

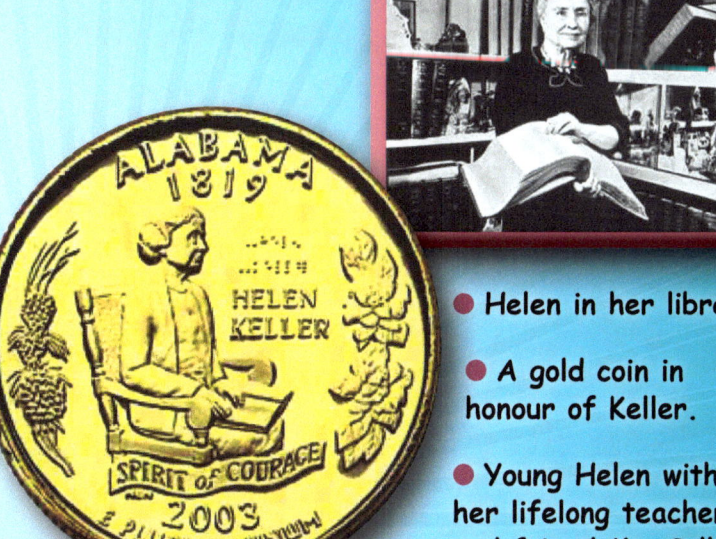

- Helen in her library.
- A gold coin in honour of Keller.
- Young Helen with her lifelong teacher and friend Ms. Sullivan.

ADE ADEPITAN

Ade Adepitan was born in Nigeria, Africa. He caught a virus at 6 months old called Polio, which left his legs damaged. He has done great things even though he is disabled, such as carrying the Olympic torch at the 2012 Olympics. He played for the UK wheelchair basketball team, helping Britain win a medal at the 2012 Summer Paralympics. Ade is also a British TV presenter and gives inspirational talks all over the world.

- Receiving an award.
- Ade playing wheelchair tennis.
- Carrying the 2012 Olympic torch in London.

Ade's parents are teachers, they saved enough money to move to the UK with him, to Newham, East London. His father had to fight for a placement in a local mainstream school.

As a child Ade didn't consider himself disabled, he thought of himself as a normal person, living a normal lifestyle. He thought anything's possible and went on to achieve his dreams. At school he was mistreated a lot but he didn't let anyone bring him down. Ade is patron speaker for wheelchair Paralympians, also a spokesperson for disabled charities.

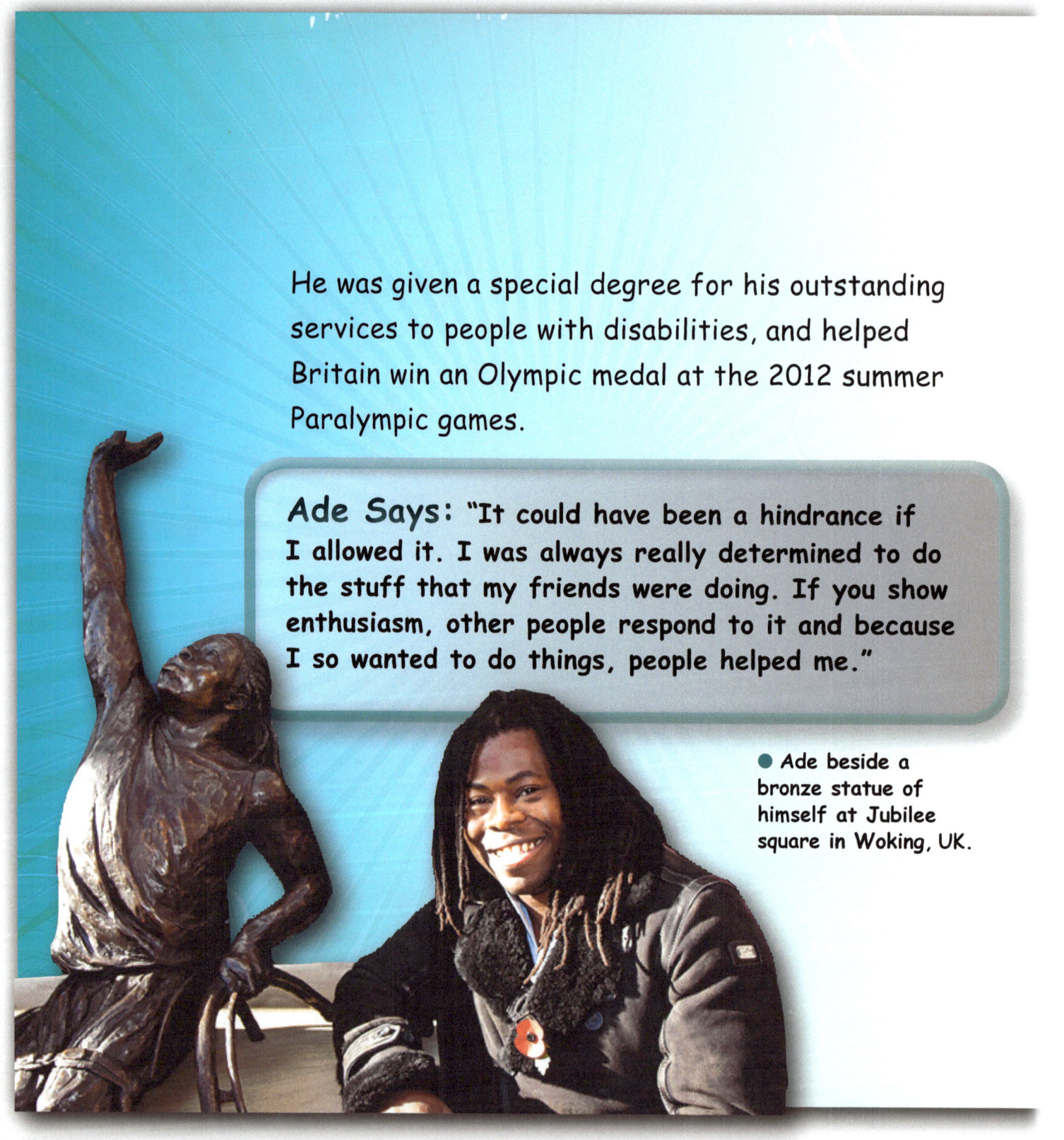

He was given a special degree for his outstanding services to people with disabilities, and helped Britain win an Olympic medal at the 2012 summer Paralympic games.

Ade Says: "It could have been a hindrance if I allowed it. I was always really determined to do the stuff that my friends were doing. If you show enthusiasm, other people respond to it and because I so wanted to do things, people helped me."

● Ade beside a bronze statue of himself at Jubilee square in Woking, UK.

I wrote about these inspirational people to make everyone who reads this book feel inspired.

These celebrities all have a disability in common, but they still believed anything's possible.

By working hard and being determined to achieve their goals.

I hope you will push yourself to achieve all you want to achieve. Whether you are abled or differently abled.

Love, Sahara Dune. xox

www.ingramcontent.com/pod-product-compliance
Lightning Source LLC
Chambersburg PA
CBHW041439010526
44118CB00002B/124